DEATH
BY ANY OTHER
NAME

DAPHNE KAPSALI

DEATH BY ANY OTHER NAME

First published in the United Kingdom in 2017

Copyright © Daphne Kapsali 2017

The moral right of the author has been asserted.

Cover by Daphne Kapsali

ISBN: 978-1544145044

For my grandmothers
Koula and Ariadne,
and for my mum.

PREFACE

It was my mum's idea to publish this book.

'Why don't you put all these stories together?' she suggested.

'What, the ones about death? How uplifting,' I laughed - but they could be.

Don't let the title fool you: this isn't a morbid book. It's a collection of stories about death and dying, yes, but death isn't morbid in itself. Death is a fact, sudden or sad, tragic or inevitable, and it can leave us bereft - but it isn't morbid. Our perception of it often is. But it doesn't have to be.

This is a collection of seven stories about death and dying, five of them new to this book and two published before, in another collection. They're a little about how we deal with death, the fact of it, and how we can never be prepared, no matter how much advance notice we have. They're a little about honouring the dead, a little about living in their honour, but mostly they're about being alive.

My stories about death are about life, after all: the life that preceded the death and how life carries on after, despite it. And that's the opposite of morbid. It might even be uplifting if you let it, if you choose to see it that way; because the dead lived among us once and that's why we miss them, and those of us who remember them are still alive.

WHERE THE THYME GROWS WILD

I can't let go of her hand. I want to. She has this way of twisting your wrist and then pulling down, which sends jolts of pain up the length of your arm, and forces your spine into a very unnatural stoop. It's no use trying to adjust the position of your hand, or let go. Once she's gotten hold of you, she engages you in a vice-like grip that's impossible to escape by ordinary means, or without causing a major incident. You have to apply for special permission to be released, stating solid and irrefutable reasons, and even then you're not guaranteed a favourable outcome. More than likely she'll swear at you and tug on your hand sharply. Experience has taught me it's best to grit your teeth and bite your tongue, wince if you must, but bear it, as she shuffles along, the walking stick she refuses to relinquish bashing against your shins, beating the rhythm of the long, slow walk.

This is taking my grandmother to the shop.

Thyme, with its ominous, silent *h*. A humble herb, more common than mud in a dry country like Greece, growing wild amidst the rocks of this rough terrain. Growing wild over the graves of our dead in rural churchyards, feeding on their bones, its silent *h* a subtle mockery in these places where there is no more time, or time is all there is.

If you run your hand over it its scent lingers, but what haunts me, what reverberates for me is the word, the sound, *thyme*, and its tacit deathly connotations. A recurring theme in my childhood, a threat dropped casually in conversation. My grandmother, laughing: 'One day, I'll be off to the fields of thyme.' Or punishing me, when I've displeased her: 'And you'll be sorry then.' I was sorry instantly, in advance. My child's mind trying to conjure up a picture of this mystical place where the thyme grows wild, that my grandmother is so fond of. Capturing only a vague sense of endless green-grey, and the lone figure of my grandmother rustling through it, walking away, already too far to catch up with; releasing its lingering scent in her wake.

We fight over who's gonna be the one hold her hand. No one wants to. We make up excuses to stay behind, some urgent need remembered at the door. 'You go ahead, I'll catch up.' It's not for lack of love, but these long slow walks with twisted wrists are excruciating. We're so focussed on the destination, on getting there, that we have no patience for the journey, for the senseless stopping and starting, for the random running commentary.

We pull on her hand irritably, quicken our steps. 'Come,' we say, 'keep moving.' Collecting sorrys for later because we think there will always be time to deliver them.

It's not for lack of love, but love is expressed in small ways and slow walks and longer patience, and not holding out your hand for your grandmother to grasp can look a lot like indifference. Retrospectively: like regret.

She won't be going to where the thyme grows wild. When she dies, she will be buried next to her husband, to have their long years together at last. She will be buried at the cemetery of Kaisariani, at the foothills of Mount Imittos in Athens, where nothing grows wild except weeds, over the old, untended graves, through the cracks in the headstones of the poor and the forgotten at the far end of the cemetery. She will be buried next to my grandfather, beneath a sombre rectangle of grey marble, in the looked-after part near the church, where stone angels keep watch over rows upon rows of middle class Athenians, and candles burn brightly through the day and night. She's not happy about this; in fact, she's violently opposed to the idea. 'Don't you dare put me next to that man,' she threatens my mum. She would prefer a solitary stroll through the fields of thyme to an eternity lying side by side with the man who left her too soon, and she can hold on to a grudge as tightly as she holds on to your hand. She won't let go.

He shimmers strangely for me, this grandfather, this half-remembered almost-man. He is an amalgam of anecdotes and snapshots, memories true and invented, stitched together loosely to create an effigy to fill the space reserved for him on the family tree, where he perches, a couple of branches above me, smiling his enigmatic smile. He is in his paintings and his sculptures that casually adorn our homes, in the ceramics and iron tools he painstakingly collected and catalogued. He is a quiet presence on the edge of a long row of much louder graves, a slab of grey marble that could do with a polish, not because he was a quiet man in life, but because there are no words or symbols or stone angels, no lanterns or garish flowers that could capture his presence or the sudden unfathomable magnitude of his loss – nor should such a thing be attempted. But my grandmother, thirty years his widow, who walked beside us in all her long life - my grandmother, in death, should have her thyme.

She takes her walking stick out everywhere we go, but it's better if there are two of us flanking her, a twisted wrist on either side. It takes some of the fear away, and her cautious steps become a little lighter. I observe the way she moves her feet, always trying to correct her, to fix her. 'It's because you don't bend your knees,' I say, frustrated at her straight-leg shuffle, with the impatient arrogance of limbs that behave exactly as I expect them to. She takes no notice of me; her walking stick bashes against my shin bone, another souvenir bruise to add to my collection. 'It's your turn on the way back,' I hiss to my sister as she saunters past.

My grandmother will have her way in the end. She will be buried next to her husband, and the grey marble will bear both their names, but I will plant some thyme on her side, wild and thorny like she is sometimes. And I will visit on and off, when the mood takes me, and pat the headstone and say 'Hey', twice now, to both my grandparents, and brush the fallen leaves off the marble. I won't bring flowers. I will water her thyme and then I'll leave and get on with my day. I won't come often. Thyme is a sturdy herb, obstinate for living; it doesn't need a lot of tending to. Neither do the dead.

It's fucked up, the nature of death, when the absolutely unthinkable is an absolute certainty. I try to imagine it, and capture only a vague sense of green-grey and the helpless, inevitable sensation of her soft, dry hand slipping out of mine. I try to prepare myself for a time when I will long for her tight, twisted grip and the long slow walks and the stopping and starting, because my grandmother is ninety and it's been years since she brought up the fields of thyme.

What a waste, to be sorry in advance. When we could walk a bit slower now and have fewer things to be sorry for later. I try to apply retrospect ahead of time, develop some foresight, because there's a part of me that can look ahead and see myself looking back, but it's an accident that teaches me patience in the end. I have a fall and strain a muscle in my calf, and walking becomes an ordeal. I get a glimpse of what it's like to need a hand to help you on your way, to be begrudged the slowness of your pace. My grandmother and I limp along, hand in hand, and I joke feebly about the blind leading the blind, but then I stumble and it is she who holds me up. I look ahead, travel forward to where the thyme grows wild, and, with that morbid kind of foresight, I understand that this will be something to look back on: my grandmother and I, shuffling along the cobbled path, clutching each other's hand while the others, the able-bodied ones whose limbs behave exactly as they expect, saunter past rolling their eyes, and how the two of us don't mind that they leave us behind. My grandmother and I, united in the slowness of our pace, taking our time despite the able-bodied ones and laughing at how our bodies have betrayed us; holding on to each other, and when my leg gives way it is she who keeps me from falling.

I don't want to let go of her hand. I'll have to. I don't know if I can.

But I know that when I do, her steps will be certain; unhurried but brisk. She won't need my hand or my mum's or my sister's, no wall to lean against, no walking stick to keep her stable. She won't look down at her feet, she won't stop along the way, she won't ask where we're going. She'll look straight ahead, to a place that I can't see, that I'm not ready yet to see, a place where the thyme grows wild, and she'll take long, swinging strides like she used to, and she'll leave us all behind, clutching sticks, leaning against walls, holding on to each other for balance as our knees go weak. And only towards the end, right at the end, maybe, she'll stop, and turn around, and wave with both hands, both hands free, because she won't need to hold on to anything anymore.

And I'll have to let go, then. I'll have to let her go.

HOSPITAL LIFT FLOOR CIGARETTES

I'm standing in a hospital lift, going down, making bad jokes and trying not to think of MRSA or the reason I am here. I wave my arms about, nervous gestures, and the precious, pre-rolled cigarette slips through my clumsy fingers and drops to the floor.

'Fuck!' I say, too loud. The other occupants look up in alarm. It's the wrong word, the wrong volume for this environment. Hospital lifts and hallways are all about whispered euphemisms and the silent voids of words not being said: this is no place for loud fucks.

I wriggle down and pick my cigarette up, with a sigh. My mum and my uncle give me wide-eyed stares.

'I'm not gonna *smoke* it,' I say defensively. 'I may not have the highest standards in hygiene, but I draw the line at hospital lift floor cigarettes.

They nod, non-smokers both, but they can see the wisdom of this line being drawn.

Other lines are the IVs that have snaked their way into my grandma's body. Putting things in and drawing things out. Medicating, feeding, removing waste. They're the lines that connect her to this world, the means by which we hold onto her. She often tries to pull them out, sudden, jerky movements of irritation or rebellion, tugging at them and swatting at the hands that interfere, but she doesn't try too hard. She's still connected. She swats at me when I try to hold her hand, but she lets me, eventually, pretending defeat. And I hold on.

I wrote about leaving as death the other day. This is death as leaving. People ask questions.

'When is she leaving the hospital?' they want to know.

'I don't think she is,' I tell them, and in the silence that follows the D word starts to form, and the question gets shortened to pre-empt it.

'Is she leaving?' they ask gently. The Greeks, like any other nation, have many gentle euphemisms for death and we whisper them to each other, so carefully, lest we disturb the sleeping beast and it claims us all.

But death doesn't sleep, waiting to be invoked by the careless speaking of its name; nor does it lurk, personified, in shadowy places, to pounce on us as we pass, oblivious, on our way to another day we take for granted. Turning it into a monster is nothing more than an attempt to tame it, just like we try to temper it with whispered words, when a loud fuck would be more appropriate.

I don't know if death is the end. It's the end of *something*, but as it relates to living, it depends on how you define that condition. Does my grandma live on, as they say, as long as I remember her? As long as my brain synapses still fire off memories that keep her in motion, does she remain alive? Is she still smiling somewhere because there are still neural pathways that lead to that image? Or is it *her* pathways that matter, exclusively, the synapses of her particular brain that have lost their spark? Does she end when those synapses go dark?

I practice saying the words out loud. 'My grandma is dying,' I say, but I don't know what it is that I'm saying. I don't know if death is the opposite of life. I don't know if it's a state, or a process, or the name we give a moment. But it's definitely a fact; the only fate we can rely on. And it strikes me now as ironic that something so monumental can be so commonplace at the same time. Because, for all our whispered euphemisms and our reverential silences, death is as common as dirt. As commonplace as leaving, or living. And living itself is full of leaving, and death; of people that you love and people that you lose, and you can't hold onto them when they want to go. No matter the reason, no matter where they're going; no matter how many lines you draw, or stick into them, there comes a time when you have to let them go. And a loud fuck, sometimes, is the most appropriate response. Because, *fuck*, my grandma is dying. There is no tempering that, for all the gentle words I could use.

Because death is no place for loud fucks, and we cannot know, as we pass it on our way to another day that we take for granted, how many of them we still have in us. We might as well get them out while we have the chance. While those synapses are still sparking and light the fires that keep us alive.

I don't mind picking cigarettes up when I've dropped them on the pavement, but I draw the line at hospital lift floors. And perhaps that's what it's all about: the lines that connect us, and the lines that keep us apart, that set the boundaries and define what is ours. And knowing where to draw them, and when to step over them; when to erase them and draw them elsewhere, and when to see them for what they are: a line that we cannot cross. And I think maybe dying, the verb, is that: drawing a line in the sand, and placing yourself on the other side.

'I don't know where I'm going,' my grandma says. Then she shrugs. 'But I don't care.' She tugs at the lines that keep her connected.

One day, soon, she'll break free and make her drawing in the sand. She's on her way out, as the English euphemism goes, and we cannot hold her. All we can do is gather at the doorway and wish her well on her journey, past the line that we cannot cross.

***

From *collected: essays and stories on life, death and donkeys* (published October 2016)

MAKE IT NOT SO

In the process of coming to terms with the end of a relationship, bargaining is a wonderfully fun stage wherein, according to Elizabeth Kubler-Ross and many other grief and mourning theorists since, all the *what ifs* truly come into their own and, no longer content with merely blowing holes into your past, start clamouring for a place in the present.

In the case of death and terminal illness (which is what Kubler-Ross' original model referred to), bargaining generally takes the form of appealing to a higher power. We throw money at doctors, experimental therapies and alternative treatments and, when that fails, we turn to distant, omnipotent (and, in many cases, long abandoned) deities and negotiate with them for a different outcome.

In my own, thankfully limited experience with death as an adult, I originally took a more direct approach and appealed to my dying grandmother herself. I would walk into her hospital room and berate her for being silly, which sometimes raised a weak smile but not our hopes. I then changed tack and took to explaining to her, patiently, that there was nothing wrong with her, that this was no more than a minor setback, that she would be fine, as if multiple mini strokes and failing kidneys were merely a matter of misunderstanding. I painted her nails red and promised her we'd go out dancing, if only she'd stop this madness and get out of bed and put her shoes on. When, in her lucid moments, she expressed a desire for something – *anything* – I'd latch onto it and promise her that thing, dangle it in front of her and hope that she'd follow me, like Eurydice in Greek mythology, out of Hades and back into the land of the living, where she could play another game of cards, take another holiday by the sea, walk down a London street beneath a low, overcast sky. But, like Orpheus, I doubted, and I would turn around at the last minute, each time, and she wasn't there. I would go back and find her where I left her, in her hospital bed, taking shallow, laboured breaths through an oxygen mask and gently shaking her head.

And then she stopped doing even that, and the bargaining began proper. I offered up everything of myself that I could think of. I would be kinder. I would be more grateful. I would never buy another pair of jeans. I looked for signs and omens everywhere and, if they weren't there, I invented them. Lacking belief in god, I threw myself at the mercy of other inexplicable and capricious forces, such as the weather, technology and public transport. If the lights turn green. If the sun comes out. If my iPhone shuffle plays a particular song. If the right bus arrives. I prided myself on being quite reasonable; I wasn't asking for a miracle, just a little more time. As though my grandmother's death was an essay due, and there were extenuating circumstances. One more week, one more day, one more conversation – that's all. 'I get it,' I'd say. 'But not yet. I'm not ready yet.' Towards the end, and even after the end, I dropped all pretence of rationality. I would squeeze my eyes shut and repeat a desperate mantra of 'Make it not so'. That was all: make it not so. But it was so. Totally, finally and irrevocably.

That's the thing about death: it's final. And in its cruel finality it contains, if not the thing itself, then at the very least the possibility of closure. For all of our negotiating, we know, as rational beings, that our position is pretty weak; we are aware that, ultimately, we are powerless against it. "Make it not so" is just a blanket we wrap ourselves in, woven of empty words, not quite a wish but the ghost of one. I'm not religious, so perhaps my understanding of this is incomplete, but I'd like to think that most of us know that the tale of Lazarus is a parable, and that bringing people back from the dead should be confined to the realm of horror movies.

But when it comes to the death of a relationship, finality is negotiable. One of the first questions we typically ask when told of a break-up is: 'Is it final?' And, as demonstrated by the vast number of zombie love affairs staggering around among us, it often isn't . Unlike death, the end of a relationship contains within it the possibility of reversal. And closure, when it eventually becomes desirable, is much harder to obtain. If we're lucky, the dying are wise and selfless enough to give us something that'll help us leave them behind. My grandma, months before her death, assured me that she'd had a great life, and that the end of it was not to be mourned. I dismissed it as morbid nonsense at the time, and it gave me little comfort when the end actually came, but I eventually recognised it as the greatest gift she ever gave me: something to hold onto, so I could let het go.

***

Excerpt from G*et the fuck over it: a literary self-help guide for intelligent people* (upcoming)

DEATH BY ANY OTHER NAME

The church bells rang this morning. It was unusual, because our church isn't normally active. The bells only ring on the feast day of St. John; for births, deaths and weddings. And yet they rang.

For whom?

For whom?

I didn't think. It was unusual, but I didn't ask. I only thought *the church bells are ringing*, and went back to my coffee.

I didn't think, but when I called Eleni, later, and she told me, I wasn't surprised.

'I know,' she said, before I had a chance to speak. 'Five o'clock.'

The funeral: Mrs. Souli next door. That's why the bells were ringing.

'I didn't know,' I said. 'That's not why I called you,' but I wasn't surprised. There was something about last night: the full moon, the high winds, the sheets flapping wildly in Mrs. Souli's yard. Something about it foretold of stillness.

Death by any other name: does it make it easier? Sometimes we use euphemisms to soften the edges of things so they don't cut so deep, so suddenly. But death has no edges, no shape, no boundaries to contain it. It isn't pliable, it's not susceptible to our words. It's neither hard nor soft: it just *is*. And *euphemism* means to give something a better reputation, but I suspect death doesn't give a shit what we think of it. So: passed away? No. Moved on? No. Gone to a better place? No. The Lord didn't call her to his side, no. She died in the night; her heart stopped. The funeral's at five. And the church bells are ringing. I finish my coffee and make another cup.

My grandma died this winter, and that's what I said when they asked:

'How's your grandma?'

'She died.'

It might sound crass, but death isn't subject to our adjectives. It earned me some funny looks, but isn't funny better than tragic? Isn't it better than pity, and the awkwardness of trying to come up with words to console the inconsolable? Death is no easier by any other name. And it's not my job to make it easy.

Here, on the island, I'm a little more careful. Careful of others, of how they will handle my grief. But it got me in trouble, this shrinking away from the words.

'Is your grandma well?' Marios asked, when I stopped by his shop.

'Um,' I said. 'Not so much.'

He stared at me eagerly, urging me to go on, but I couldn't bring myself to say *dead*.

'Well. You know.'

He brought his hands up to his face, lowered his voice. The words came out slowly. 'Is she gone?'

'Yes,' I confirmed. 'She's gone.'

They say this a lot here: *gone*. I adopted it the next time, and got into trouble again.

'How's your grandma?' said Flora, at the supermarket in Kamares.

'Gone!' I replied, almost enthusiastically, because I knew the answer this time.

'Oh,' she said. 'Did she go far?'

'Quite far.' A little concerned about the way this conversation was turning.

'And who's chasing after her?'

'No one!' I cried, panicking now. 'No one's chasing after her! We let her go!'

'Oh. You mean *gone* gone.'

'Yes. Completely.'

'Not just her mind.'

'Nope. All of her!'

We looked at each other, then, and laughed. And then had a brief philosophical discussion about life and death. Life, which should be as funny as we can make it. And death, that can be funny too, sometimes. Not euphemistically: for real. Laughter is a privilege of the living.

I didn't go to my grandma's funeral, but I go to this one. It's not a ritual that means anything to me, but her son, Manolis, has red-rimmed eyes and I can tell he appreciates the brief squeeze of my hand on his shoulder. It's probably the first time I've touched him. I have an urge to hug him, but I don't. I go to the funeral, instead.

At the church, I light a candle and stick it in the sand, where all the other candles burn at different heights, jostling for space in the waiting room for god's ear. Wishes, prayers, regrets; tokens of duty, tokens of faith. Flames burning in her memory, in her name, but she has no use for either. She is nothing, now, that we can understand. We cannot call upon her like we used to when we walked past her door. Her name is a broken line, and memory is a thing of the living.

I light my candle but I don't cross myself. There are enough crosses in here to make the numbers up. I find a step to perch upon, between the candle stand and the door, my skin tingling from the heat of the flames on the left, a light breeze cooling me from the right, and I watch the people come in. There's a good turnout; no doubt this will be remarked upon, several times, in the days to come. It will be repeated in service of her memory, offered along with "she's resting, now" and "at least she didn't suffer", as consolation. The useless balm of human kindness on a cut made no less deep by the euphemisms. Her good reputation; her popularity, on this day of her death.

In the middle, in a strangely-shaped box: nothing. Not a person gone too still, but something that has never known motion. Not stillness, but the absolute absence of anything. A person is an animate creature; when it stops moving, terminally, it's a person no more. Nothing, in a box, wearing a dead woman's clothes, adorned with flowers. It might sound crass but that, to me, is consolation: that she's not here. She is elsewhere, or nowhere, but not here. Not in this box, with its force field of respectful distance and hands clasped together, pressed against our bellies, to protect our essence from the death in our midst. That's comfort, more than "gone to a better place"; she had her place in this life, among us, and now she's gone. There is no box that can contain her – any of us – in death or in life.

How do you behave at a funeral? Do you smile when you see people you know? Do you nod solemnly? Do you blink in acknowledgement and then lower your gaze? And for whom? For whom? Who cares?

Not the dead. The dead don't need anything from us; they are no longer anything, they are no longer anywhere that we can understand. They don't hang around to make judgements of our behaviour, they don't linger over these empty boxes, counting flowers and crosses and working out whom to haunt. They can see right through our careful expressions; they can see right through us all. To them, I think, *we* are the ghosts: flimsy, gossamer-thin shadow puppets, performing our lives, overestimating how substantial we are. Arranging our faces on behalf of the dead, but it's our own reputations we're looking after. And if we're haunted by anything, it's our regrets, burning away like votive candles. We keep them burning.

The priest speaks at the end. He says words of praise, words designed to offer comfort; he speaks of Mrs Souli's role in this community, the husband that she lost too soon, the son whose name lit up her face in a smile, every time. He speaks of how she was loved, and I feel bad, because I didn't love her. I feel bad as I balance, stiffly, on my perch, with arms folded across my chest, trying to resist my own resistance to this ritual and be here for the right reasons: for Manolis, for his gentle, understated grief, for whatever it means to him that the girl next door turned up. And then I notice that I'm crying, and it takes me by surprise: I didn't love her, but she touched my life, briefly, just as I touched her son's shoulder this morning. It meant something, after all.

It was the sheets that gave it away. I didn't have a premonition, only knowledge in hindsight. I didn't love her, but I knew her, and the sheets would never have been left flapping that way if she were still around. She knew these winds, she knew these clothes lines: she had her standards. She barely knew my name, and she was as baffled by me and my fancy tinned goods as I was by her, but she appreciated my presence next door. 'The neighbourhood has brightened up,' she'd tell me. 'I can see your lights on, and I know you're here.' Side by side, I chased after solitude as she chased loneliness away, and we shared a winter, her and me, with lights burning bright to chase away the darkness. We had no language to speak to each other, but we kept our lights burning to say *I am here*.

The dead don't need anything from us; it's the living that need our kindness. All we can do for the dead, if we feel that something must be done, is to use the privileges of the living. To laugh, and cry, and ring the bells and turn up when we're needed. To find our better place in this life, and live it in the most uncontained way possible, and be more careful of the memories we make than the memories we'll keep. To look after each other instead of our reputations. And put out the candles that we have no use for, and turn on our lights, in the dark of night, and brighten up the neighbourhood and say *I am here*. And touch people when we can, even lightly, even briefly. It means something.

***

From *For Now: Living a deliberate life* (upcoming)

KEEPSAKE

My mum says maybe it's because of the anniversary of my grandma's death that I feel like this today. 'Maybe your body knows,' she says, but I can't remember the date. It may have been the thirtieth or the thirty-first of July, and it was only five years ago and I've looked it up every year since, but I cannot remember. I know – I think – it was a Friday night, and that the funeral was on the Monday, so I can go back in time, into my calendar, like I've done every year since, and look it up, the last weekend of July 2011. I can find out the date, again, but I don't think I want to. There's a reason, there must be, that I forget every year.

I wasn't there when she died but, then again, neither was she. That's why I was able to leave; that's how I gave myself permission to. She wasn't there to be there for, and I didn't have it in me to stand by an empty bed any longer, waiting for the body to catch up with the soul, and for our hearts – our aching, cowardly hearts – to accept it.

She had put in appearances, in the weeks running up to the end, the long, slow weeks of hospital hallways and the disinfectant hand gel that I'd become obsessed with. She'd show up, sometimes, and so would I, to sit by her bed and hold hands that were at once, paradoxically, swollen and diminished, to paint her nails red, inexpertly and in defiance of the nurses who wiped them clean overnight and told me off in the morning – bright red, for who my grandma had been. For the spark that still lit up her eyes, sometimes, when she shifted up on her pillow and raised her head and sent us away, out there, into the world at the end of the hospital hallways, the bright, sunny world that we could still be part of. When she told us not to waste our time, because she never had. My grandma had used up all her credits in this life – but deliberately, joyfully; she had always been a gambler, a card player, but she was in it for the game, not for the win. And she knew when the time was right to stand up and leave the table: she wasn't one to linger when the game was up, stripping herself of valuables for one last chance. She had taken all the chances she'd been given, and now she was out.

"Pass," she kept saying, round after round, but we didn't listen. We didn't want to. The game was over and still we kept throwing our valuables onto the table, watches and jewels and promissory notes, piling our hopes up onto an empty bed. Her appearances became rarer and rarer as the weeks went on and eventually she stopped showing up at all. And I didn't have it in me to wait when I knew, despite myself, my cowardly heart, that she wasn't coming back. She was gone long before I left, and she had given me permission. So I came to Sifnos while my grandma lay diminishing in her hospital bed in Athens, and carried on living while I waited for her to die.

She died in a hospital bed in Athens and I wasn't there. The body finally caught up with the soul and stopped pretending to be occupied, and as her heart monitor stopped counting beats, our cowardly, still beating hearts began the process of acceptance. Release: perhaps that's what it was. For her and for us. And it may well have been five years ago today, that Friday night that I received the call, but I don't know and I don't want to know. There is a reason I keep forgetting. Because you remember a person for who they were when they were there, living their life beside you, and how stupid, how wasteful to try to scrunch up that life into a single moment of death, and make that your keepsake. I will keep her as she was, alive and sparking, and leaving the game with all her jewellery still on, and her nails painted, expertly, bright red.

And maybe it is, as my mum says, that my body remembers, or maybe the way I feel – slow, strange, blinking stupidly in the bright, sunny world like I used to after each of my hospital visits

– is just a symptom of being alive. A reminder that there is still a bright and sunny world out there, at the end of the hallway, that I can be part of.

***

From *For Now: Living a deliberate life* (upcoming)

IN A WORLD WITHOUT GRANDMAS

I dreamt that my grandma hadn't died, after all. That it was a mistake, a misunderstanding, that we'd misplaced her, somehow; somehow failed to notice that she'd fallen down the back of the sofa and, while we thought she was gone, she'd been there all along, trapped between the cushions like a ring that slipped off your finger or a trickle of loose change. And then somebody moved something and there she was, not lost, after all, and laughing at me and with me both, entirely true to life.

That my grandma is dead might be a mistake in philosophical terms, but that's as far as my interpretative thinking can take me. Not to where she is, not reaching between the cushions to find her, perfectly preserved and unharmed, and put her back where she belongs. She doesn't belong here anymore, I understand. Entirely true to life, and no half measures: my grandma went from living to dead and when she died, she died completely. If she had only been a little bit dead or only dead in part, that would have been a very frightening thing. Although, saying that, there are people all around me that go through their lives a little bit dead, and they don't seem to notice that anything's wrong.

Dying doesn't erase us. The marks we make, our scribbles of a life, the hieroglyphics that we carve or ink or trace on loose sheets of paper and hardbound, hand-stitched tomes, school desks and park benches and cubicle walls, across the sky or, if we're lucky, across another's heart: death doesn't erase them, the marks that meant we were here. But death puts an end to the scribbling. Time's up, pens down everybody: whatever you've got, it'll have to do. Hand your life in now, and be on your way.

She scribbled all over me, that woman: my grandma. Both of them did. And I miss them both now, individually and collectively, as the concept of grandmas, now that they're both gone. There is something about a world without grandmas, something desolate, the irretrievable loss of a comfort that only they could provide – even if they weren't the cuddly granny type, which neither of mine were. They were both feisty, fierce, magnificent in their own ways, so completely alive and putting their mark all over us in places we couldn't even begin to imagine, until they stopped. But they were grandmas, nonetheless – *my* grandmas, mine. And there are times when the only calls I want to make correspond to those two numbers that are still in my phonebook but not to the voices I long to hear. There are times when I reach for the phone before I remember. Before I understand, again, anew. What death means.

What death means: time's up. But time goes on, for me, in this world without grandmas. I cannot find the comfort now, I cannot reach between the cushions and pull it out – the soft, loose skin, the warm, dry cheeks, the smell of cooking and the tupperware boxes to take home, care packages stuffed full of cigarettes and roasted nuts, weird trinkets given randomly and random, weird advice, the phonecalls to berate me for not having called and the unmasked, unmitigated pleasure when I did, husky voices and irreverent remarks, twinkly eyes and cascading silver hair and expensive perfume, the easy smiles and the words of love – all the love – that, from the safer distance of a generation gap, they were never shy to express, and the strong clasp of a bony hand that will never let you go, until it does. All the scribbles and the marks that make up my experience of grandmas, those two that were mine: it's written all over me, but the comfort is lost. I cannot reach it. I can move cushions around all I like, I can tear the things to shreds and knock the sofa over, but I will not find what I'm longing for, in a world without grandmas. It's not a misunderstanding. That is what death means.

But maybe I can look to those scribbles and those marks and remember what *they* mean; how they mean that my grandmas were here, and they were mine, and they were magnificent. Maybe I can look to them and find the precedent, the will to be magnificent, in their absence, in my own right, and to be alive fully, not a little, not in part, but *completely*, while I'm still allowed a pen to scribble with and there are surfaces on which to make my mark.

***

From *For Now: Living a deliberate life* (upcoming)

NAMEDAY

That night, the night we saw May, my granddad ordered fried courgettes in addition to our usual salad and chips. I knew the reason why; I had been expecting a gesture like this. We took a slice each, chewed on it self-consciously, remarked upon its flavour, and how it was complemented by the grated cheese sprinkled on top. The other words were left unsaid. Our morbid celebration expressed in deep-fried, battered vegetables.

It was my grandma's nameday. Mine too; I was named after her. The story goes that she had forbidden my dad from naming any child of his after her, passing on the curse of her horrible name. But in 1970s Greece, where church and state shared a bed at night, a Christian baptism was not merely the process by which every Greek infant was given its name and welcomed into the bosom of the Orthodox church; it was compulsory. And the Church, in turn, frequently refused to baptise a child under a pagan name; you had to be named after a saint, or not at all. Daphne, as it turned out, was no saint. An alternative was sought, and a compromise reached and, against my grandma's wishes, I became Daphne Kyriaki, a middle name to pacify the priest and infuriate its original owner. The curse passed on, but once removed. Trapped between a first and last name, neutralised, like a dormant gene.

Saint Kyriaki was the miracle baby of a devout, childless couple. She was named for the day she was born: Sunday, the day of the Lord. Kyriaki was very beautiful, and many suitors sought her hand in marriage, but she was betrothed to Christ. This was the first century A.D., and Christians were not all that popular, especially good-looking ones who obstinately refused to surrender their virginity, and Kyriaki attracted some unwelcome attention. She was martyred for her faith and died a virgin at age 21.

Ominous precedent aside, Kyriaki is an old fashioned name, a name that was never in fashion. Its diminutive, Koula, is pretty bad, too, part of a trend for shortening the more austere sounding names to make them softer, somehow. If Kyriaki is stiff and humourless, Koula is approachable and cheery. My grandma hated both, but opted for the latter, as the lesser of two evils. But she wasn't happy about it. It was her cross to bear, her own bit of martyrdom, and she bore it good naturedly, as befits a Koula, except when admonishing my dad for defying her.

'Poor child,' she'd say. 'I wouldn't wish that name on anyone.' It was the only topic on which she conceded my dad had done wrong.

She needn't have worried. The curse had been neutralised, and my middle name was never used: I was never Kyriaki. I was always Daphne and my grandma was always Koula. Motherhood had provided a respite, the person she spent most of her time with addressing her, exclusively, as "mum". But then I came along, crazy namesake child, and decided, with simple, faultless logic, that her name was Koula, and that's what I'd be calling her. Her curse became my charm, a happy word, invoking an adult who indulged my every whim and fed me exotic food such as smoked salmon and caviar and Heinz Baked Beans and Hershey's Chocolate Syrup, which came in a squeezy bottle and which I was allowed to squirt directly into my mouth.

This must be said for my grandma: she was exceptionally good at holding a grudge. Besides which, she was obstinate as hell; I've never known her to back down on anything. If my calling her by her name had softened her towards it a little, she wasn't about to let anyone know. If she came round to the idea of there being two of us, if she began to like it, she would hardly even admit it to herself. Which makes what happened all the more strange.

My dad says that birthdays and namedays were rarely celebrated when he was growing up. He remembers Christmases and Easters, abundant feasts of multiple courses served on fine dinnerware; my grandma was the perfect combination of natural hostess, talented cook and unashamed but discerning glutton, the latter of which three qualities she bequeathed directly to me. My dad's own birthday was observed annually, his nameday sometimes remembered and sometimes missed, until 1984, when it became immortalised in family lore by my sister's birth on the same day. My grandparents' birthdays and namedays, however, were never remarked upon. Perhaps they were celebrated quietly, in private, but they never featured on the family calendar.

My grandma was especially determined not to have any fuss made about her. None of us ever knew, for certain, her date of birth until we saw it printed on her hospital wristband, in the final weeks of her life. If pressed, she would admit to being a Pisces, but refused to divulge the actual date. She would mumble something deliberately incoherent, in the hope of putting you off; if you insisted, as I often did, she would literally swat you away, like a fly.

'Oh, leave me alone, will you?' she'd say. Jovially, and with an infuriating half-smirk of private amusement. But with finality. And then she'd change the subject.

But, for some reason, she suddenly began calling me on our nameday.

It happened, without prelude, when I was six. My dad passed me the phone.

'It's our nameday today,' my grandma said. 'Did you know?'

I didn't. I thought my nameday was on Palm Sunday when, according to scripture, Jesus' path into Jerusalem was strewn with laurel leaves by the faithful; the tentative link being that the Greek word for the laurel plant is Daphne. My parents had decided I should have a nameday, and I didn't qualify for All Saints.

'Your other name,' my grandma clarified. 'Kyriaki.'

The phonecalls became annual, and were always invested with a faint trace of irony, the sense of a joke exclusive to the two of us. And so my grandma relented: I was Daphne every day of the year, except on the 7th of July, the feast day of Saint Kyriaki. Also, in 2005, the day of the London bombings, and the one time, since that first call, that my grandma and I did not speak; all UK mobile networks were down. She forgave me, begrudgingly, on account of the bombs.

She never backed down on the topic of her birthday, however. I remember that date printed on her wristband. That is, I remember seeing the date, and the act of committing it to memory, storing it away, triumphantly, for that day in March, next year, when I'd finally be able to call and wish her *Happy Birthday*. I remember holding her wrist in my hand, and how light it felt when I lifted her arm a fraction to reveal, at long last, the elusive numbers that curled round to the underside of the band. But I just cannot, for the life of me, remember the date itself. It's a strange thing. Perhaps my pragmatic mind erased it when it understood that call would never be made; perhaps it recognised, with the cruel detachment of intellect, that this information was already obsolete. But I suspect it was something different: a sense of fair play. My grandma had not revealed the date herself; she had not fallen for my ploys or my pleading. A card player to the last, she had never shown her hand. Some nameless nurse, unwitting participant in our game, had given her away. If victory was mine, it was an empty one. Let history record the true winner, in all the ways that count: Koula, my grandma, a Pisces; date of birth unknown.

I lie: 2005 wasn't the only time. There was also 2012, when my granddad called in the evening, to reproach me, in the gruff tone he'd adopted in the last few months, for forgetting my grandmother's nameday. I hadn't; I'd spoken my wishes to her in my head, but to call someone else in order to acknowledge, mutually, that she was no longer there to call was more than I could take. There was 2013, when I thought I'd learnt my lesson and called him in the afternoon.

'It's Koula's nameday,' I said. He had forgotten, and all I'd managed to do was upset him.

And then this year, the 7th of July 2014. The night of fried courgettes, and May.

May was my grandma's best friend. I remember the two of them together, a double act that defined the summers of my childhood. Their smokers' coughs, their smokers' laughs, their husky smokers' voices. Their dirty jokes, but always on the right side of tasteful. They always sat close together, their elbows almost touching, waving ever-present slimline cigarettes about as they gesticulated wildly, indiscriminately enthused by any topic they happened to pick up. Dressed in almost identical outfits of borderline garish kaftans and Jackie O sunglasses, as was the fashion; their perfectly manicured fingernails always painted red. May was blonde, the slightly rounder of the two, big boned and big haired; my grandma darker, more petite and less impressively – though still immaculately – coiffed. They were ladies of a certain class, a certain generation, married to prominent men, real men, with excellent breeding and military careers, who drank malt whiskey and played bridge. Modern, fairly liberal for their time, but firmly rooted in the traditions that defined their role as women, their role as wives. Aware that it was a role, and performing it to perfection.

Except in the afternoons. The impossibly long summer afternoons, those endless hours between 2 and 5 – the forbiddingly named "Hours of Public Silence", when the men took their siesta, and the children should be neither seen nor heard. When my parents were around, they'd insist on putting me to bed, but in their absence, my grandma and May let me stay up. This was Girls' Time, and I was one of them, they said. This was when the real talk happened. They huddled together on the sun-baked patio of our rented summerhouse, smoking cigarettes and trading secrets in low, excited whispers, in compliance with Public Silence, though a burst of laughter often gave them away. I had no idea what they were talking about, but they made me feel included, and I would happily sit there and bask in the warmth of their company as the hours drifted past. I was almost disappointed when 5 o'clock came, and I was released to join the other children for a swim.

In the first few years, it was my grandma who called on our nameday. I was still a child, and she was still pretending those semi-covert calls were made for my sake. Later, when I crossed into adulthood and moved to London, the roles were reversed by tacit agreement, and I was the one who made the calls. The content, however, was unchanged. We'd exchange wishes, call each other Kyriaki, always with that edge of irony, and then move on to other topics.

'I miss you,' she'd tell me, in English, before hanging up. She often said that when we spoke on the phone, she in her kitchen, preparing dinner in a housedress and curlers in her hair, or getting ready to go out for a game of cards, and I in whichever London flat I was calling home at the time. 'I miss you, as they say.' *They*, I presume, were the English, my adopted nation (often referred to, with a hint of sarcasm, as "your friends, the English", when one of them, commonly a politician, did something to piss her off), who had stolen me away; a move she approved of but lamented for the distance it put between us. And *I miss you* was always said in their language, but with no attempt at an English accent, each letter enunciated sharply, as though she was reading out the phrase transliterated into Greek. I don't know why. Though we never disguise our affection, ours isn't a family that ends calls with words of love. We send kisses across the phone lines, and love is implied. Perhaps, paradoxically, the foreign words made saying it less foreign, somehow.

I had played it safe this year. I had called the week before, and suggested we meet. I didn't mention the date.

'Monday,' I said. 'Are you free?'

I figured, if he remembered, we'd be spending the evening of my grandma's nameday together; if he forgot, it would be dinner, as usual.

Before my grandma's death, my granddad and I had never spent any time alone. Now, almost three years on, we were still negotiating the terms of this new relationship that had been thrust upon us. He had become quite difficult, embittered by loneliness and unpredictable in his grief, and I, in turn, had pulled away, unsure how to relate to him in the absence of my grandma. We had established certain rituals – this restaurant, the same dishes every time – and we adhered to them to get us through.

This night, by the time we finished our starters – the chips, the salad, the memorial fried courgettes – we had already exhausted our standard topics of conversation: my work, my sister, my mother's health, the last time either of us had spoken to my dad. My granddad cast around desperately for something to say. He failed, and summoned the waiter instead, to order his usual half portion of meatballs.

'And a nice steak for the young lady,' he added, with but a cursory glance in my direction, both a man used to ordering for women, and a grandfather keen on pleasing his gluttonous granddaughter.

And then his gaze fell on something behind me, and his face lit up.

'Niko!' A man materialised by our table, mid-eighties, a few years younger than my granddad. He had a bustling, jolly manner about him, and was accompanied by an attractive, but much more reserved woman, with a neat short bob. Pleasantries were exchanged and introductions were made. I shook their hands, and sat back down. The newcomers were shown to their table, and my granddad rejoined me at ours. But he was restless.

'Tell me,' he called across to the now seated Nikos, 'is George joining you? And May?'

Yes, Nikos confirmed. George and May were on the way.

My granddad nodded. 'I'll be very glad to see them,' he said and, with obvious effort, turned again to face me.

'George and May?' I said. 'As in...'

'The Papadopouloses, yes. You remember them?'

'You were close friends. You used to see a lot of them.'

'We did.'

'What happened? Don't you see them anymore?'

He shrugged. 'We grew old. After a certain age – it isn't easy. People tend to keep to themselves.'

A commotion at the entrance interrupted him, and my granddad bounded out of his chair with an agility I hadn't thought I'd see again. Once up, he seemed at a loss about what to do next, so he just stood there, between tables and chairs, this 92-year-old man of six foot three, who had fought in wars, like a shy child waiting to be noticed.

'George! Look who's here!' Nikos called out, and then everyone was in motion, shaking hands and remarking on the marvellous coincidence that brought them together. I stood up then, and sought May. A couple of steps behind George, whom I wouldn't have recognised out of context, she was unmistakable. She wore a slightly passive expression, which changed completely when our eyes met. We gravitated towards each other.

'Oh,' she said, up close. 'Well. There you are.' Surprised and unsurprised, at once. She kissed me on both cheeks and held my gaze for a long moment. And then, without another word, she drifted away to join her friends.

Our mains had arrived, but my granddad had no interest in his meatballs. He was perched on the edge of his seat, half-heartedly moving food around on his plate, while I worked on my steak.

In an unprecedented lapse of good manners, he turned his whole body around, and sat sideways in his chair, staring eagerly at the foursome now ordering their food. He was like a puppy straining on his lead. George must have noticed.

'Spyro,' he shouted, 'join us.'

'Oh,' my granddad said, as if this were entirely unexpected. 'Thank you. I'll just wait for Daphne to finish her meal.' But he was already on his feet.

I looked up at him.

'I'm done,' I said. 'Let's go.'

'Shall we?' he asked, without waiting for a response. 'But it'll be the men talking,' he added. 'You can sit with the ladies.'

May motioned to a chair next to her, at the end of the table.

'Smokers' corner,' she said.

I sat down and tried not to stare. May looked the same; slightly puffier, perhaps, bloated by age and medication, but largely unchanged, given the twenty years that had elapsed since I'd seen her last. Her hair was arranged in her trademark bouffant. All that was different was her expression: the mischievous twinkle that had danced across her face when she was with my grandma conspicuous in its absence. I glanced down at her hands: her nails, at least, were reassuringly red.

In the hospital, I did battle with the nurses over nail polish. I kept painting my grandma's nails red; they kept wiping them clean. I'd come in each day to find my efforts had once again been removed overnight. Something to do with needing to monitor the colour of her fingernails, they said. A perfectly legitimate medical reason, I'm sure, but they didn't understand that, with their nightly interventions, they were stripping away a lot more than nail polish.

I had never seen May without my grandma. At first, the presence of one only highlighted the absence of the other, and there was a fleeting, guilty thought of things being the other way round. But then, with a jolt, I realised I was wrong: May wasn't alone.

I hadn't been to my grandma's grave since the day we buried her. She wasn't in that casket we lowered into the ground, and her name on that slab of marble made no sense. My granddad, her husband of sixty years, had failed to invoke her for me, and she hadn't lingered in the home they shared for two thirds of their lives. She wasn't tethered to any object or place. But she was here this night, this 7th of July, sat between her old friend and her granddaughter. May had brought her along.

May didn't say much. She asked me a couple of questions, remarkable in the detail they contained, the minutiae of my life that she recalled. When, on a couple of occasions, Nikos' wife asked me something, May supplied part of the answer herself. She had kept up with my news all this time, the only gap the last three years, when the reports had ceased. I realised, conversely, how little I knew about her; I didn't even know if she and George had kids, or grandkids. I suspected she wasn't very well; her cough had a strained, chronic quality to it, and at some point George glanced at his watch and passed her a pill. But I couldn't ask about that. So I mostly kept quiet, and watched the men talk. George and Nikos were loud, jovial men, constantly shouting things at each other and their wives across a table laden with food.

My granddad, in sharp contrast, sat quiet and dignified, his hands folded on his lap, a benign smile on his face. I could tell he was struggling to keep up, but he looked happier than I'd seen him in years.

'Do you want to go?' he asked at some point. 'Are you bored?'

'No,' I lied. 'We'll stay as long as you want.'

Unexpectedly, our evening had turned into a celebration, after all, and a feast to match my grandma's tastes. Endless dishes were passed around from hand to hand, making their way around the table. When the fried courgettes reached our end, May scooped two slices onto her plate.

'Your grandma was crazy about these things,' she said, with something of her old twinkle passing briefly across her features. 'I've seen her polish off an entire plate on her own. Right here, in this restaurant.'

'Happy memories,' George interjected, having caught her last phrase.

May nodded. And then she put her fork down, and left the courgettes on her plate, untouched.

'I remember one summer,' she said a little later. 'You must have been five or six. Right after your parents split up.'

'Eight, then. I was eight.'

'Koula cornered you, and told you your father was having a very hard time and you mustn't do anything to upset him. She made you cry.' Her eyes creased up in a smile, as she shook her head. 'And then your father came into the room and gave her the greatest bollocking I've ever witnessed.'

'May!' my granddad chided, wincing at her language.

'Happy memories,' George said again. 'After all this time, when you look back, everything is happy memories.'

May ignored them both: this story was not for their benefit. She looked straight into my eyes, and it was a summer afternoon again; this was the women talking. We dissolved into giggles, our amusement entirely out of proportion with this place, this time. Between us, unseen, my grandma rolled her eyes and pretended to take offence at this blatant attack on her personality.

Once we had regained our composure, May lit a cigarette and leaned in close.

'You know, Koula, she never put anyone above your father. Not even you. But she loved you. You came a very close second.'

Not long after, my granddad and I stood up to leave. As he made his way around the table, shaking hands, I lingered by May. I searched for words.

'It was so good to see you,' I said. 'Really.'

She nodded, and I almost walked away. But the words hadn't been right. I put my hand on her shoulder. Touching my grandma, almost, once removed. 'Seeing you,' I tried again, 'I remembered Koula. Not that I don't remember her every day,' I corrected myself, 'but – you know.'

May placed her hand on top of mine. 'Yes,' she said. 'I know.' We stayed like that for a few seconds, until my granddad, halfway to the door already, dangled his car keys at me.

'Well, goodbye,' I said, and made to leave.

But Nikos looked up at me, eyes narrowed, and titled his head.

'You look like your grandmother,' he observed.

'Yes,' I said. 'Perhaps. From a certain angle.'

'And it's Koula's nameday today,' my granddad offered, from the doorway.

'Of course,' said George. 'Saint Kyriaki.'

'And mine too,' I blurted out, to break the silence that had descended upon the table. 'I was named after her.'

May caught my eye. She mouthed the words, *Happy nameday*, as they were hastily repeated out loud by everyone else, their relief at having a living person to direct their orphaned wishes to palpable.

'But wait,' Nikos piped up, addressing my granddad now, 'I thought you said her name was Daphne?'

'It is,' I replied, 'on every other day. Today, I'm Kyriaki.' I gave no further explanation.

At the far end of the table, huddled close to May, my grandma winked. And with a nod towards her friend, she indicated she was staying. As I had known she would. She held up her hand, a cigarette burning away between her fingers, showing off nails painted red again. I raised my own hand in response, in farewell.

'I miss you,' I told her. In all the languages.

My grandma smiled as May nudged the plate of fried courgettes, subtly, in her direction.

***

From *collected: essays and stories on life, death and donkeys* (published October 2016)

Thank you for reading!

If you have enjoyed this book,
please take a moment to rate it,
or write a short review on Amazon.
Honest reader reviews are the best way
to support independent authors.
And they make us very happy!

Thank you!

Other things you can do:

If you like my work (so far),
check out my other books on Amazon.

Keep in touch by
joining my mailing list
for polite and infrequent
updates, news and special offers.
(No spam. Never ever.)

You might also like to sign up for
my Advance Readers' Team
and get all my new books for free
before they're released.

Or send me an email through my website:
www.daphnekapsali.com

ABOUT THE AUTHOR

Daphne Kapsali is a writer, reluctant yogi, pathological optimist and dedicated coffee drinker - among many other things. In 2014, she gave up her life in London to spend the autumn and winter writing on a remote Greek island called Sifnos; the result, a book entitled *100 days of solitude* – 100 separate and interconnected stories on claiming the time and space to live as your true self and do what you love – was published in March 2015 and has become an unexpected bestseller. She has since published another five books, all of which are available from Amazon.

Daphne is a big fan of the law of attraction, the universe and all things positive, and hopes her story will keep inspiring others to overcome their fears and limiting beliefs, and live their best lives.

She and her multiple personalities divide their time between London and Sifnos, where they argue good-naturedly about who is more qualified to run their life. They have yet to reach a conclusion.

Get in touch:

Website: daphnekapsali.com
Blog: 100daysofsolitude.com
Facebook: facebook.com/daphnewrites
Twitter: @dafiniduck

18324710R00036

Printed in Poland
by Amazon Fulfillment
Poland Sp. z o.o., Wrocław